Original title:
The Existential Crisis Chronicles

Copyright © 2025 Creative Arts Management OÜ
All rights reserved.

Author: Nathaniel Blackwood
ISBN HARDBACK: 978-1-80566-007-1
ISBN PAPERBACK: 978-1-80566-302-7

A Flight Through Doubt's Abyss

I boarded a plane of thoughts so wild,
With baggage of questions, some silly, some mild.
"Is life just a ride on a carnival train?"
I chuckled with fear as I tried to explain.

The pilot was my mind, clearly confused,
Flying loops and curves, feeling quite bruised.
"Do I steer or just sit? Where are we going?"
My thoughts raced around, a chaotic flowing.

The clouds were my worries, fluffy and gray,
The seatbelt of reason kept slipping away.
"Will I crash into fate or soar with delight?"
Laughter erupted; I would be alright.

As we zipped through the air, I spotted a sign,
"Overthinking Zone: Watch Your Mind's line!"
With a grin on my face, I took a deep breath,
For life's absurd dance is a sweet kind of jest.

When we landed on ground, my worries dissolved,
In the garden of chaos, I found my resolve.
"So here's to the flight, filled with giggles and doubt,
Life's comedic ballet, let's all join the bout!"

Paradox of the Wandering Mind

I ponder deep, yet stay afloat,
Like fish who swim, but can't take note.
Thoughts chase tails, a furry race,
In circles round, I lose my place.

A coffee cup my guiding star,
My dreams are loud, my thoughts bizarre.
I question life with every sip,
Then spill my doubts on my own trip.

Fragments of a Fragile Self

A puzzle piece lost in the sky,
I'm just a bird with a shrieking cry.
My mirror shows an awkward face,
Reflections dance in a clumsy pace.

My socks mismatched, my hair askew,
Who am I? A jester or the glue?
Chasing laughs with every thought,
Scribbling notes in a coffee pot.

In Search of Meaning's Ghost

I chase the ghost, it's quite a tease,
It hides behind the latte trees.
Questions float like confetti rain,
But meaning's playing hide and gain.

Do socks feel joy? Does dust have dreams?
While I'm just lost in endless schemes.
I trip on truths that don't exist,
Yet still, I dance to my own twist.

The Abyss Within

I peep inside the void's embrace,
With rubber ducks in a serious race.
The abyss chuckles, quite absurd,
As I ponder life, a silly bird.

My thoughts are like a circus tent,
Where all my worries find content.
With every laugh, I lose a thread,
Yet wear it proudly on my head.

A Dance with Absurdity

In a world where socks don't match,
I wear mine with flair and a scratch.
Fish in bow ties glide on the floor,
Who needs sense? I'm here for more.

I tap my toes on the ceiling high,
While eating cake, I wonder why.
Is my cat plotting an escape?
He winks at me; it feels like fate.

Jumping on clouds made of whipped cream,
Why be serious? Life's a dream.
Juggling thoughts like clowns with glee,
Who cares if nothing feels quite free?

So let's dance with whimsy tonight,
Laugh with the shadows, twirl in delight.
Embrace the odd with a silly grin,
For in this chaos, we truly win.

Shadows of Questioning

Why is a raven like a writing desk?
No one knows; it's a ridiculous quest!
I ponder deeply, then eat a snack,
These questions hang like a fruit that's whack.

The moon tried to text me last night,
But I was busy, oh what a fright!
My thoughts are like noodles in a pot,
Twisted and tangled; are they worth a shot?

I asked a toaster if life's a joke,
It popped up bread and began to smoke.
Is this enlightenment or just charred toast?
I'll take my wisdom from ghosts, at most.

In shadows I dance, round and around,
With laughter and questions that seldom are found.
A parade of quirks, absurdly clear,
In this circus of doubt, I shed every fear.

Threads of Uncertainty

I knit my thoughts with yarn of doubt,
But every stitch unravels, no clout.
My sweater's a riddle, a puzzle too,
One arm is brown, the other is blue.

Rabbits in hats do a curious jig,
While I contemplate a marshmallow pig.
Should I care if things make sense,
When logic's just a jumbled pretense?

I spoke to my shoes, they said "Let's walk!"
But all we did was sit and squawk.
Unique adventures in mundane wear,
Life's absurdities float in the air.

So I'll stitch my doubts, each patch a flare,
Sending colors of chaos into the rare.
With threads of uncertainty, we'll cheer and sing,
In a tapestry woven, the bizarre is king!

Beneath the Surface of Being

Beneath the surface, what do I find?
A potato wearing a hat so blind.
"Am I real?" it asks, with a quirky twirl,
I chuckle and say, "Let's give it a whirl!"

A pickle debates with a wise old shoe,
"Is the sky really as blue as our stew?"
Questions bubble like soda pop fizz,
In this realm of nonsense, now that's the biz!

A rubber duck floats in existential glee,
"Quack philosophy! What's it to me?"
I join the parade of absurdity bright,
Exploring the depths of a humorous night.

So let's dive down where the giggles reside,
In this ocean of madness, we'll take a ride.
With laughter beneath, and joy in the air,
Who needs answers when life's so rare?

The Weight of a Thousand Thoughts

My mind's a circus, oh what a sight,
Clowns juggling worries in the pale moonlight.
Should I floss tonight or order a pie?
Life's big questions make me want to cry.

Buffoons parade with thoughts so absurd,
Does the dog dream of chasing a bird?
I trip over shadows of decisions made,
While pondering ice cream flavors that fade.

In a world of chaos, I sip my tea,
And wonder if squirrels are judging me.
Invisible whispers guide my fretful dance,
As I giggle at life's strange happenstance.

So I'll wear my hat, both stylish and grand,
With a feather of doubt, the best I can stand.
Balancing dreams on the tip of my nose,
Juggling sanity while friendship bestows.

A Soliloquy in the Night

Under a blanket of shimmering stars,
I ponder time, like counting on Mars.
Why is my toaster so set on my fate?
Would it toast me if I were late?

The fridge hums softly, my nighttime muse,
Whispering secrets I can't quite refuse.
Is the cat judging me from the floor?
Her eyes seem to say, 'What's life for?'

I check the clock, it giggles at me,
Why does it move so hungrily?
Drifting through thoughts like clouds in a dream,
The night laughs with me, or so it would seem.

So here in the dark, I ponder the light,
And if I should dance like a fool, tonight.
Curtains of worries, let them all fall,
Tomorrow's a puzzle, and I'll solve it all.

Sketches of Fleeting Reality

Life's a quick sketch, a doodle on page,
Filled with scribbles of worry and rage.
What if I'm just a ghost in the mix?
Making bad choices, doing old tricks?

With crayons of doubt, I color my fate,
Yet somehow I'm happy, isn't that great?
My rubbery dreams bounce back when they fall,
Sketchy existence, but I'm having a ball!

In moments of chaos, I paint my delight,
With every mishap, I giggle at fright.
Life's an abstract, a curious tease,
Like socks that get lost in the dryer's an ease.

So grab your brush, let's smear joy around,
In this gallery of nonsense, fun's abound.
Reality winks, it's just a ruse,
Laughing at us, as if to amuse.

Whispers of the Forgotten

In the attic of memories, dust starts to speak,
Echoes of laughter and silly antique.
Should I wear my old shoes that pinch?
Or wade through the day on life's crooked inch?

The past swirls around like a dancing ghost,
Should I toast to the days I miss the most?
Nostalgic giggles that tickle my brain,
As I trip down a path of laughter and pain.

Mirrors reflect what's too hard to see,
A parade of faces smiling at me.
I ponder the wisdom of age with a grin,
While my laundry piles higher than my hopes ever been.

Let's raise a glass to the days that we've spent,
To the wacky adventures and time we lament.
For in this chaos, we find our own way,
Life's a fun riddle, let's dance and delay.

Constellations of Our Thoughts

In a galaxy made of dreams,
We ponder while sipping our creams.
Stars form shapes of our wild despair,
Like a pizza slice in mid-air.

We count sheep but they don't respond,
They're busy plotting ways to abscond.
Is this mind or just a joke?
A cosmic dance, or funny smoke?

Our worries swirl like dancing dust,
Lost in thoughts that we can't trust.
Do we exist or just recycle,
Our whims in a cosmic cycle?

So let's toast with laughter and cheer,
To thoughts that vanish like a sneeze near.
In this circus of absurdity we play,
Who knew pondering could be this cliché?

A Journey Through the Unseen

I packed my bags for nowhere fast,
With thoughts as heavy as my breakfast cast.
Maps of 'why' and 'what if' in tow,
But directions? Well, they're a no-show!

I wandered through a field of 'maybe',
Found a tree that looked quite hazy.
Its leaves whispered, 'Just let it be,'
But I'm still stuck here sipping my tea.

My compass spins with a mind of its own,
Leading to places I've never known.
Is that clarity or just a mirage?
This journey is starting to feel like a collage.

But laughter echoes in every space,
As absurdity becomes my saving grace.
A journey through humor, twists, and turns,
In this unseen world, a giggle burns!

The Art of Non-Being

In the gallery of thoughts so grand,
We paint with colors we can't understand.
Non-being hangs in frames of glee,
Who knew emptiness could be so free?

We sculpt our fears like silly clay,
Mold them into shapes that play.
A bust of doubt, a statue of cheer,
Artistry thrives in the dear old fear.

Each brushstroke is a laugh out loud,
Masterpieces born from an awkward crowd.
In this art studio, chaos reigns,
As we giggle at existential pains.

So come along and paint your plight,
With hues of humor, dark and light.
In the art of non-being, we all can find,
Comedic treasures left behind!

Dusk of Certainty

At dusk we gather with furrowed brows,
Debating if we should take a bow.
Certainty fades with the sun's last wink,
Leaving us pondering with a clink!

Let's raise a toast to what's unclear,
To questioning everything we hold dear.
A wise man sighed, 'What does it mean?'
As his cat looked wise, smug, and serene.

Maybe the world is a giant riddle,
Plucked on strings like a nonsensical fiddle.
With laughter echoing through the night,
We'll dance in shadows, feelings light.

So here's to dusk, uncertainty's friend,
Where clarity comes and goes like a trend.
In the twilight of reason, let's just embrace,
The absurdity wrapped in this cosmic space!

The Garden of Question Marks

In the garden, questions grow,
Fluffy doubts with nowhere to go.
Sunshine laughs at thoughts that roam,
While weeds whisper, "Are we alone?"

Each flower blooms with a puzzled face,
Roots tangled in the crazy race.
Butterflies flutter, not quite sure,
If they're flying or a daydream tour.

A gnome thinks hard, tipsy on wine,
Says, "Is life just a long punchline?"
Rabbits nibble on thoughts that sprout,
While the roses pout, "What's it all about?"

Bumblebees buzzing existential cheer,
"Is this real, or just a weird sphere?"
Every petal, a riddle to find,
In the garden of so many minds.

Migrations of the Troubled Mind

A brain on the move, where to go?
Thoughts hitchhike on clouds, all aglow.
A flock of worries takes to the skies,
Chasing horizons, where logic lies.

The mind's like a train, off the rails,
Chugging along with whimsical tales.
Passengers whisper, "Is this the end?"
While the conductor seems more like a friend.

Pigeons coo wise words from afar,
Saying, "It's better to just be bizarre!"
Migratory dreams flit without a map,
Each stop brings a new, silly trap.

From the nests of doubt, they take flight,
Gliding through hues of day and night.
In the chaos of thought, joy can be found,
Migrations of minds spinning 'round and 'round.

The Pulse of the Unlived Life

In the rhythm of dreams yet to bloom,
Lives not lived dance in a cluttered room.
The heart beats fast, but what does it hear?
A symphony of might-have-beens, oh dear!

Sticky notes clutter the mind's old desk,
Plans scribbled 'til they're quite grotesque.
A goldfish swims circles in borrowed time,
Singing out loud, life's a funny rhyme.

Chairs are empty where we could have played,
And laughter echoes in decisions delayed.
Yet in the silence, a giggle floats by,
"What if we're all just trying to fly?"

Underneath the skin, a jester resides,
While the clock ticks life out like wild rides.
The pulse thumps loud for all that we seek,
In the untraveled path, today's usique.

Shattered Reflections in Glass

A mirror cracked, what do we see?
Fragments of self, absurd as can be.
One piece laughs, while another just frowns,
Playing hide and seek in fractured towns.

Reflections scatter, each one a jest,
"Am I the worst, or just the best?"
A mosaic of thoughts, absurd and bright,
Chasing shadows in the pale moonlight.

Glass you can't trust, it's often too sly,
Winking back with a mischievous eye.
Every shard holds a secret or two,
Each slice of insight is poking fun too.

In this carnival of introspection,
Masks reveal and hide our affection.
With every glance, we're likely to laugh,
At shattered selves, our own autograph.

Flickers of Forgotten Dreams

I woke up today, what a sight,
Socks that don't match, oh what a plight!
My dreams took a flight, somewhere high,
They left me here, just to sigh.

I chased them down the hallway wide,
But all I caught was a cat's pride.
It flicked its tail and gave a glance,
As if to mock my lost romance.

I pondered hard with coffee in tow,
Did dreams really matter? I didn't know.
A pop tart popped, and there it was,
A memory sweet, just because!

The toaster chimed, a joyful cheer,
It brought me back from the brink of fear.
I chuckled at thoughts that once felt grand,
Now crumbs of laughter float, unplanned.

Symphony of Solitude

In the quiet, I play a tune,
An opera sung by my trusty spoon.
It clangs and clinks, a classic sound,
As I juggle thoughts that swirl around.

The walls listen close, they nod their heads,
While I debate if I'd prefer to be wed.
To solitude or a partner in crime,
A dance with a mop, sounds just fine!

My plants sway gently, they get my vibe,
While I sip on tea, oh what a tribe!
Their green leaves nod, as if to say,
"Quit stressing now, just enjoy the day!"

A symphony sweet of teacups and dreams,
All performed with soloist screams.
Here's to the quirks and laughs amassed,
In my little world, forever vast.

Dances with Dread

I woke up with a jump, oh dear!
Did I forget all my plans for the year?
The laundry's a mountain, the dishes a sea,
Yet here I am, laughing at me!

My socks on the floor do a waltz,
They giggle and taunt, "It's your fault!"
I dance through the clutter, a carefree sight,
Spinning with dread, what a delight!

An existential tango, a jig on the side,
With every misstep, I just glide.
What if I trip on this crazy road?
I'll laugh it off, that's how I'll load!

The clock ticks on, but I have my way,
With each little wobble, I greet the day.
Embracing my chaos, let it spread wide,
In this dance of life, I choose joy as my guide.

A Canvas of Questions

What is the color of a thought, I muse?
Perhaps it's purple, or maybe it's blues.
A canvas blank, just waiting for brush,
But here comes the cat, in a mad little rush!

A splash of reality, oh what a scene!
Where awkward meets funny, and in between,
Questions abound, like bees in a hive,
"Am I really me, or just a live?!"

I pick up a brush, paint a grin,
What do I gain if I never begin?
With each stroke I giggle at things I inquire,
Creating a masterpiece of my own quirky fire.

The world feels absurd, and that's quite fair,
As I mix up the answers, full of flair.
So here's to the questions that never grow old,
On this canvas of laughter, let stories unfold!

An Infinite Loop of Questions

Why am I here, or am I there?
Can I be seen if I'm not there?
Do cows ponder life's deep plight?
Or do they simply moo at night?

What's the point of socks, I ask?
Do they enhance the daily task?
If trees fall down with no one near,
Does the sound ever reach our ear?

Why do we drive on the right side?
Is left so bad, it must be denied?
If I say, 'Why?' does it mean I'm wise?
Or just another fool in disguise?

The more I think, the more I trip,
In this thought loop, I can't find grip.
Maybe the answer's just to dance,
And let the questions take their chance!

Bitter Fruit of Reflection

I looked in the mirror, what a fright,
Is that a shadow or my insight?
The wrinkles laugh, they tell no lies,
"Embrace the chaos!" it slyly replies.

I ponder fruit, so juicy and sweet,
Yet it rots on the ground, a sad defeat.
Perceptions sour as lemons here,
But lemon meringue still brings good cheer!

I tried to be wise, I tried to be bold,
But wisdom tastes like beans left cold.
I guess that's life, it's all a game,
And bitter fruit will bring no shame.

So I'll wear my quirks like badges bright,
Laugh at my troubles, dance in the night.
For every sour, there's sweet to chase,
And with each giggle, I find my place.

The Horizon of Uncertainty

There's a hill I see with no clear end,
Is there treasure or just a bend?
With every step, my confidence shakes,
Is life a dance or just mistakes?

The horizon winks, it teases me,
"Come find the proof, or just let it be!"
But what's that shadow, lurking there?
A sign of hope or just despair?

Each path I take, there's something new,
A pie shop here, a zoo shows too.
Do I keep walking or head on back?
With every choice, I start to crack!

Yet laughter echoes through the breeze,
I trip over roots like falling leaves.
So here's to all the uncertain trips,
And finding smiles on our own slips!

Tales from the Edge of Perception

At the edge of dawn, I found my muse,
Telling tales from a world I'd use.
Did cats plot to take over the sun?
I swear they giggle, oh what fun!

Reality bends like a spoon, oh fine,
Is that the moon or just my wine?
I saw a shadow whisper my name,
Promised me laughter, a life to claim.

The edge of reason, a tightrope walk,
Will I soar or just get lost in thought?
With every giggle, my fears decrease,
In the chaos, I find my peace.

So here's to tales spun wild and free,
At the edge where we want to be.
For perception's just a funny ride,
Hold on tight, enjoy the slide!

The Weight of Invisible Chains

There's a heaviness I can't explain,
Like I'm carrying all my leftover pain.
With thoughts that bounce like a rubber ball,
I wonder if my brain just hit a wall.

I try to run, but I trip on my shoe,
Life keeps sending me riddles anew.
I dance with shadows, they lead me astray,
And I can't seem to find my way today.

I laugh at my plight while I sip on tea,
Why does existence feel like this to me?
All my deep thoughts get tangled like hair,
Yet here I am, lost in a world that's unfair.

Am I alone in this babbling spree?
Or is everyone just as nuts as me?
I'll laugh it off with a wink and a smile,
Who knew being lost could be so worthwhile?

Chasing Fleeting Moments

I raced with the clock, but it skipped in glee,
Every tick was a tease, "Come chase after me!"
I plucked the petals of each passing hour,
But they wilted like hopes in a summer shower.

Sunlight flickers, a mischievous glance,
"Catch me if you can!"—oh, what a dance!
I reach for the laughter, it slips through like sand,
Wishing I could live these days unplanned.

Happiness flits like a butterfly bold,
One moment it's warm, then it's freezing cold.
So I spin round and round with an empty gaze,
Life's just a series of awkward displays.

So here I am, in a fleeting affair,
Chasing moments that vanish in thin air.
I'll write my haikus with a hint of despair,
For every giggle hides a whisper of care.

Labyrinth of Lost Identity

Who am I today? A jester, a queen?
A fog in my mirror, a ghost on the screen.
I wander through mazes of thoughts that confuse,
Trying each mask, I'm just picking and choosing.

Woke up in a t-shirt that feels like a lie,
Put on a smile, but I can't tell you why.
In layers of "me," I've lost the real rhyme,
Like a clock without hands, running out of time.

Am I the hero or simply the fool?
Arguments drape me like a heavy school.
Every reflection's a riddle I chase,
Yet I find no answers in this endless race.

So hang tight, dear self, as the world spins around,
In this comedy show where sanity's drowned.
Let's laugh at the chaos, the puns we disguise,
For deep down, we're all just a mix of surprise.

Musings of a Conflicted Heart

My heart's in a tug-of-war with my mind,
One says, "Be cautious," the other, "Be kind."
Like a cat in a tree, I don't know which way,
Every decision leads me further astray.

Chocolate or salad? A choice that's so tough,
One brings me joy, the other—well, rough.
I giggle at woes while they twirl in a dance,
Like a ping-pong ball lost in my own trance.

Do I love this chaos or do I just fret?
Life's a wild taxi with no way to get.
I wave at my heart as it wrestles the night,
What a funny tug-of-war in my head's spotlight.

So here's to the conflict, I raise up a cheer,
For every laugh shared, there's always a tear.
Let's embrace the absurd while we pick our own parts,
And learn that it's okay to be conflicted at heart.

Chasing Shadows at Midnight

In the dark, I chase my fears,
They giggle and disappear,
What's that noise? Just the cat,
Or is it my much crazier hat?

Midnight snacks and midnight thoughts,
Life's puzzle with too many dots,
I ponder if socks have a mate,
Alas, they just sit and wait.

Ghosts of plans that often fell,
Dialing up my inner cell,
Is that laughter or a scream?
Who made life a twisted dream?

So I dance with silly fears,
While laughing through the years,
As the moonlight leads my way,
I'll spin and twirl till break of day.

The Symphony of Discontent

A melody of missed alarms,
Playing through my daily charms,
Piano keys and dishware clash,
And I hear my life's grand splash.

Each day's a note that bends and sways,
Tripping on my Monday haze,
The rhythm's off, but who can tell?
I'm a maestro in this shell!

Solo acts of woe and cheer,
Like my coffee that's gone clear,
A tune of chaos, sweet and sour,
With a crescendo every hour.

In this concert of my mind,
I find the fun that's hard to find,
So I'll laugh off every fall,
And dance like no one's there at all.

Echoes of Tomorrow's Dreams

Waking up to echoes loud,
Yet my dreams are far too proud,
Chasing them, they vanish quick,
Like shadow puppets, they play tricks.

Tomorrow's hopes, a funny jest,
They tease me like a persistent pest,
Am I to laugh or to cry?
Perhaps just wave my dreams goodbye!

Napping under sunny skies,
While grand plans make a great disguise,
I'll write stories of my plight,
Dancing with what feels just right.

In this game of guess and roam,
I'll find a way to make it home,
With giggles echoing through my night,
Tomorrow's dreams still shining bright.

Portraits of a Reckoning Heart

In a gallery of silly fears,
I hang my heart with joyful tears,
Each canvas made of gold and grime,
Posing for the silliest crime.

I paint my troubles oh so wide,
With vibrant shades of humor's tide,
Witty brush strokes, bold and stark,
Make every shadow sing and spark.

Framed by laughter, my heart does race,
In the spotlight, I find my place,
Each portrait tells a tale so grand,
Of tricky paths and dreams unplanned.

So here's to art that swirls and spins,
To embracing where the joke begins,
With every brush, I'm more alive,
In this gallery, I learn to thrive.

Whirlwind of Existential Musings

I wondered if my socks know,
Why they hide, where'd they go?
Maybe they're in a cosmic twist,
Dancing with fate, I can't insist.

Do fish ponder their next swim?
Or do they just make it on a whim?
What's it like to flap about,
In a world where no one's left out?

I chuckle at the clouds so high,
Do they laugh as they float by?
Do they think about the rain they shed,
Or are they just fluff in their fluffy bed?

So here I sit with my coffee cup,
In this wild whirl, I can't give up.
With each sip, I ponder my plight,
Maybe I'll nap 'til it feels right.

Navigating the Fog of Life

Fog rolls in, I squint my eyes,
Searching for sense in a world of lies.
Is this a path or a cosmic joke?
Perhaps a riddle that makes me choke.

I met a tree that gave me advice,
It whispered, "Life's not always nice."
But standing still in misty lore,
Made me question, what's life for?

Owls hoot wisdom from the dark,
But I'm still lost in a park.
Do they wear glasses to see through night?
Or wing it like we do, in fright?

A squirrel passed by, giving me tips,
"Just jump around and embrace the slips!"
His little dance made me smile wide,
In this fog, we all must glide.

The Interrogation of Reality

A pencil questioned why it writes,
"Is this my fate, or just delights?"
As paper listened with a sigh,
"Maybe we're all just here to fly."

The chair asked, "Am I just support,
Or a throne in this silly sport?"
The table shook with laughter grand,
"Reality's just a band's blind stand!"

While shadows snickered in the gleam,
"Do we have purpose, or just dream?"
They jived and jostled across the floor,
In this farce, who could ask for more?

So here I wait, a curious muse,
In a world where we all might lose.
Maybe it's better to laugh and dwell,
In questions that ring like a playful bell.

Melodies in the Silence

In the quiet, echoes sway,
What if silence had its say?
In whispers soft, they'd croon a tune,
Singing secrets beneath the moon.

A pause plays games in the air,
Tickling thoughts that wander where?
Do moments hum a gentle laugh,
Or are they just a photograph?

Crickets chirp in night's embrace,
In their symphony, I find my place.
Do they ponder their little song,
Or dance in bliss, where they belong?

Between the gaps, the melody grows,
Life's a concert, as everyone knows.
So let's embrace the quiet cheer,
And dance with laughter, loud and clear.

Threads of an Unraveled Narrative

In a world of tangled strings,
I found my socks in two different rings.
Pondering life while lost in thought,
Who knew laundry could be so fraught?

Questions swirl like leaves in fall,
Do goldfish dream or have a ball?
My cereal talks as if it knows,
Why does my kitchen have so many woes?

I tried to pick a favorite tune,
But ended up humming to the moon.
As I sip my questionable tea,
Who's really the master, you or me?

Yet laughter rings in this strange dance,
As I search for socks in a second glance.
Unraveling thoughts like yarn in hand,
At least my cat seems to understand!

Beyond the Edge of Certainty

Staring at the clock, it's just past noon,
I wonder if squirrels hold a secret tune.
Should I wear my hat or let it go?
Ah, decision-making, what a show!

I ponder life while baking bread,
But end up with cake instead.
Flour coats my hands like a ghost,
I'd be better suited for toast!

My plants are judging, leaves a-wag,
They whisper softly, 'You're a drag.'
Each petal thinks it knows the score,
Yet they wilt when I leave the door!

So here I am, a wanderer bold,
In the land of choices, both hot and cold.
But as the sun sets behind my chair,
I giggle at life—what a bizarre affair!

The Void Beneath the Surface

I looked within, found quite the mess,
A sock drawer filled with existential stress.
Do my thoughts tango or take a nap?
The void beneath is a curious trap!

Beneath my bed, what lurks in wait?
Monsters or just a misunderstood fate?
It's either a witch or just my old shoe,
I'll go with the story that feels more true.

In the fridge lies leftover dread,
Taking up space where dreams once fled.
Pasta of ages, something has died,
Yet it bleeds funny bones when I tried!

So I laugh at the chaos, I throw up my hands,
Life's made of jokes and rubber bands.
Inside the void, I find the cheer,
Just don't ask about my last dinner here!

Monologues of the Disquieted Heart

Oh little heart, so disquieted and brave,
Tell me, do you wish for a fancy wave?
With drama and flair, a grand parade,
Why can't you settle for just lemonade?

I talk to my feelings like they're old friends,
We share laughter as the night descends.
'Life's a carnival!' I shout in glee,
Except the rides are a mystery to me.

Do butterflies worry or sip sweet tea?
I'm wrapped in thoughts that cease to be.
With monologues too long, they outstay their flight,
I urge my heart: 'Let's not start a fight!'

So here we dance on this silly stage,
A tango of thought, a comedy page.
With giggles and sighs, my heart sings near,
Creating a symphony way up here!

Paradox of Purpose

I woke up with a plan in mind,
But then the Wi-Fi went down, oh so unkind.
Questions about meaning danced in my head,
Like socks missing their pair, or a cat that's fled.

What's the point of chasing dreams so vast,
When I can't find my keys and I'm late to the cast?
Perhaps I'll just nap, let the world twirl,
After all, being lost is quite the pearl!

The coffee is strong, so why am I weak?
I ponder my life while I munch on a leek.
A twinkle of wisdom, a flash of delight,
In searching for meaning, I ordered a fright!

So here's to the chaos of life's merry dance,
Between existential dread and my dog's romance.
I laugh at the paradox, sip my drink slow,
Who knew the quest for purpose could feel like a show?

Beneath the Surface of Silence

In the quiet of thought, where the echoes reside,
I find a laughing ghost that I cannot abide.
He rolls his eyes at my ponderous ways,
Quipping, 'Life's just a game; don't you just play?'

Silence wraps round like a cozy old coat,
Yet I hear it snicker, like a joke meant to gloat.
It whispers absurdities, secrets untold,
As if the universe is just trying to mold.

So I dance with my musings, tiptoe on air,
Every thought like a bubble—I stop and I stare.
The depths of my silence echo with cheer,
As I argue with shadows, a witty smirk near.

What's the meaning of it all? I shrug and I grin,
For beneath every stillness, there's chaos within.
With each wink from the void, I laugh and I say,
In silence is laughter, life's silliest play!

Fleeting Moments of Clarity

A flash of insight in a morning fog,
Is that a lightbulb or just my old dog?
For every grand thought, there's a silly mistake,
Like thinking I'm deep while I'm just wide awake.

The moments of clarity come in a blink,
Followed by laughter—what's next? I can't think!
Like a squirrel chasing nuts beneath my bed,
I ponder the meaning then go back to bread.

A spark like a firework bright in the night,
Only to fizzle and fumble from sight.
I pen down my wisdom, my musings too clear,
Then lose it all quickly—where's my last beer?

Yet here's to those flashes, however they fade,
The giggles of insight, the plans that we made.
Life stumbles and tumbles, a comic old show,
In fleeting moments, it's laughter we sow!

Through the Veil of Uncertainty

Behind every question, a curtain does drape,
I squint through the fabric—wait, is that tape?
The answers keep dancing, just out of my reach,
As I trip on my thoughts like a slippery peach.

I wear my confusion like a stylish old hat,
With feathers of doubt and a cat that just sat.
Each moment a puzzle, I fumble in jest,
For clarity's a riddle, and laughter's the quest.

Oh, uncertainty, you cheeky little sprite,
You turn every ponder into a laughing fight.
Yet in your wild dance, I find quite a thrill,
Like sipping hot tea while riding downhill.

So cheers to the mysteries that keep us awake,
To comedies woven throughout our mistake.
With humor in hand, we'll navigate the gray,
Through the veil of uncertainty, we'll laugh all the way!

Questions Carved in Time

Why do socks vanish, oh so sly?
Is the universe just a cosmic pie?
I ponder my purpose while I sip a brew,
And wonder if cats think aliens are true.

Do fish get thirsty in their watery realm?
Or is it humans who drive the helm?
I scratch my head at the thoughts that invade,
Like a fruit fly party that won't ever fade.

If a tree falls and no one's around,
Does it make a noise, or just hit the ground?
Maybe it whispers secrets to the air,
While squirrels gather and act like they care.

In my mind's circus, the clowns take their seats,
Juggling questions, oh what a feat!
With laughter as armor, I march through the day,
Delighting in riddles that dare lead me astray.

The Language of Silence

Silence speaks louder than a thousand shouts,
Yet here I am, filling in doubts.
With a grin and a shrug, I bask in the void,
Where existential dread feels oddly devoid.

What language do ducks use when they quack?
Is it deep philosophy, or just a light snack?
Between bread crumbs and random quirks,
I find wisdom in birds with funny works.

Sitting on benches, I watch life zoom,
Carrying dreams like balloons in a room.
Do thoughts have weight, like a loaf of stale bread?
Or are they just whispers inside my own head?

In a world full of chatter, I silently grin,
Catching giggles from deep within.
A riddle, a chuckle, an existential jest,
In the theater of silence, I find my rest.

Kaleidoscope of Consciousness

A kaleidoscope spins with colors so bright,
Reflecting my thoughts in a dance of delight.
Do stardust dreams twinkle in fractured rays?
Or are they just pixels from yesterday's maze?

What if my brain is a disco ball?
Spinning reflections of nothing at all?
With each twist and turn, I trip through the day,
Finding joy in chaos that giggles away.

In my mind's gallery, odd paintings hang,
Of ice cream mountains and telephone clangs.
Questions whirl like confetti in the breeze,
Floating through moments, with awkward ease.

But who's got the map to this zany land?
When logic is nonsense, and nonsense is grand.
I laugh at the puzzle, the colorful mess,
In the fabric of thought, I love to confess.

Realities Unraveled

In dreamland's fabric, realities twist,
Where unicorns dance and shadows enlist.
Do clouds have parties when no one can see?
Or do they just sulk, sipping tea with a bee?

Layers unwrapped, like a birthday surprise,
Each moment a trinket beneath the skies.
Why do I trip over thoughts in my head?
Like a clumsy ballet on a stage made of tread?

If worries are ghosts that give me the fright,
I'd summon a laugh, banishing night.
Ticklish conundrums from dreams that unfold,
Casting laughter like spells, bright and bold.

With giggles as armor, I wander and roam,
Through this whimsical maze that feels like home.
Embracing the chaos, I'll dance with a smile,
In a world where absurd can stretch for a mile.

Chasing Phantoms of Self

In a mirror, I see a face,
But is that really me in place?
My socks don't match, what a delight,
Perhaps I'm just a ghost tonight.

Chasing shadows, what a chase,
Lost my keys in empty space.
I grin at chaos, all is well,
This body might be on sale.

Lost in thoughts, they wander free,
My brain's a circus—come and see!
I wave to thoughts that came and went,
Is my real self in the tent?

Phantoms howling, what a show,
They laugh at me, but I just glow.
In this chase, I dance and skip,
Who knew sanity was on a trip?

Echoes of Sorrowful Lullabies

The moon hums low, a song of woe,
As shadows skip, it's quite the show.
My dreams are like a leaky boat,
Drifting softly, lost afloat.

Once I wished for things so grand,
Now I'm here with dessert in hand.
Chocolate cake can ease the pain,
Who needs peace when sweets remain?

Echoes whisper of time that flies,
Yet I'm still here in my disguise.
With every bite, I question life,
Is it all just cake and strife?

Lullabies of sorrow sing,
But oh, sugar makes my heart spring.
In this chorus, I'll join the fun,
Life's absurd—let's eat and run!

The Veil of Ordinary Days

Today I wore mismatched shoes,
Not sure if I'm winning or lose.
The toaster burned my breakfast cheer,
Another day, I simply sneer.

Ordinary? Quite the charade,
Waking up feels like a parade.
Zombie-like I brew my tea,
It screams, but it's fine by me.

I scribble plans in ink so bright,
Only to lose them—out of sight.
My to-do list laughs at my plight,
"Stay ordinary," it says, "It's right!"

But ordinary can be a jest,
In chaos, I find my quest.
So here's to days with coffee spills,
Where simple joys give crazy thrills!

Lost Voices in the Labyrinth

Wandering through a maze of thought,
Lost voices echo, are they bought?
I ask for help, they giggle loud,
Who knew confusion draws a crowd?

Around the bend, I meet a friend,
We share our woes, it never ends.
He thinks he's real, I play pretend,
Two lost souls—what a blend!

A sign says, "Exit," such a tease,
But all I find are musty bees.
"Pollinate your brain," they buzz to me,
A sweet distraction, can't you see?

In this labyrinth of silly strains,
I laugh to hide the tangled chains.
Together we'll roam, trumpets in hand,
Lost voices singing through surreal land!

The Fragile Fabric of Being

Threading thoughts with a twist of fate,
I ponder my snack, should I tempt my plate?
The universe sighs as I eat my fries,
Is there more to life than this fast-food plight?

In socks mismatched, I prance about,
Wondering if purpose hides behind the scout.
The cat looks bored, as if he knows,
That wisdom's lost with my wardrobe woes.

I tripped on my dreams, they were hard to find,
Danced with my shadow, it's one of a kind.
Yet I laugh at the mess, my robe's on backwards,
In this tangled dance, I'm all sort of fractured.

But hey, I'm still here, in my chaotic way,
A fragile thread in this cosmic ballet.
So grab a donut, we'll spin in glee,
Finding joy in the strange absurdity.

Portraits of a Perpetual Wanderer.

Each step I take feels a tad unsure,
With a map upside down, can I find the door?
The path's a riddle, as I munch a snack,
Is it just my mind, or am I off the track?

With shoes so scuffed, I roam this sphere,
Collecting odd looks, and a hint of cheer.
Each stranger smiles, as if they know,
The wandering heart, it's a curious show.

I chat with squirrels, they seem quite wise,
Pointing out nuts while I analyze.
Could I be lost or just on a quest?
To find out where chaos feels like rest?

So here I go, in this mockumentary,
Sketching my life, oh, what a gallery!
With laughs as my compass, I won't despair,
In wandering ways, I find my flair.

Whispers in the Void

In the silence loud, I hear them speak,
Voices of nothing, oh what a freak!
They talk about snacks, then fall very still,
Should I be worried, or just have a thrill?

With each tick of time, the clock makes a jest,
What's the point of this endless quest?
I raise my glass to the ghosts of doubt,
Cheers to the whispers that float all about!

The void's not empty; it's filled with my thoughts,
Like socks in a dryer, oh what a knot!
Yet laughter erupts from the depths I find,
Dancing with echoes—a curious mind.

So here's to the whispers, crazy and spry,
They tickle my brain and make me ask why.
In a world so bizarre, I'll toast to the whims,
Finding humor in nothing, my joy never dims.

Echoes of Forgotten Souls

In a room full of echoes, I wave to the past,
Did I forget something? I'm not sure, at last.
With a grin in the mirror, I check my hair,
Are these ghosts laughing, or is it just air?

I step on the toes of memories bright,
As shadows chuckle in the dead of night.
This crowd of phantoms, they dance with glee,
A party of spirits just waiting for tea.

So what if I'm rambling? It feels quite divine,
Conversations with echoes are simply benign.
They nudge me to ponder the things I regret,
But laughter erupts, so I don't fret yet.

With each silly thought, a smile I draw,
Even echoes agree, I have no flaw.
So let's raise a toast to the souls that we miss,
In this comedic life, I find pure bliss.

The Tiara of Uncertainty

Woke up today with a crown of doubt,
My brain's a circus, there's chaos about.
Should I wear socks? Should I wear shoes?
Existence is tricky, oh, what to choose!

Coffee or tea? It's a crucial toss,
Each sip's a gamble; will I be the boss?
Flip a coin, make it quick, oh dear,
Life's a loud comedy, yet I still fear.

The mirror laughs back, it knows my plight,
A jester's reflection, what a weird sight.
Who needs a tiara when perks are at stake,
In this grand old circus, my life's just a fake!

So I twirl on my throne, a crown made of fluff,
In this fun house of thoughts, it's never enough.
With laughter as armor, I may just survive,
Uncertainty's dance keeps the spirit alive!

Beyond the Veil of Comfort

Peeking out from my cozy nest,
The world outside looks like quite the test.
Should I step forth? Will my coffee hold?
Or should I retreat to my blankets of gold?

The couch has whispered sweet nothings to me,
"In this bubble of bliss, you're totally free."
But beyond its hugs lies a laughter-filled space,
Where socks mismatch and I sprint in a race!

Dared to venture and tripped on a cat,
Fate's little prank, oh, how funny is that?
In the realm of comfort, I tend to recline,
But what if adventure pulls on my spine?

So I flip-flop around, like a fish on dry land,
With each quirky step, life gave me a hand.
It's funny how comfort can feel like a trap,
While giggles and snorts hide beneath every flap!

Lost in the Silence of Existence

Sat in a chair, something feels off,
Quiet's a monster that seems fit to scoff.
Why is the toaster so smug and so gray?
It pops out my bread but with no word to say.

I ponder the stars, they blink and they tease,
In this soft cosmic void, I hear nothing but bees.
My thoughts wrestle hard with the threads of the night,
Even silence has giggles; there's a joke in this fight.

Each tick of the clock sounds like laughter or moans,
I play peekaboo with my thoughts, seeking tones.
Do echoes have sound? Or just giggle in hide?
In this quiet wonder, I mock and abide.

So here I float, like a balloon in a tree,
Caught in the silence, it's laughing at me.
With a wink from the void, I dance through the grey,
Existence is funny, in its own quirky way!

A Journey Through the Intangible

Packed up my bags with socks filled with dreams,
Into the great unknown where nothing redeems.
What if I find that I'm really just air?
Guess I'll float through the void like I just don't care.

Met a ghost in the alley; he offered me tea,
Said, "You're not alone, well, at least not with me."
Haunted by laughter, we danced in a swirl,
He talked about life like it's an exciting whirl.

Items unseen hold the weight of our hearts,
Like mysteries wrapped in a set of fine arts.
So I juggle my whims like a clumsy old clown,
An intangible dance; watch me twirl and fall down!

My journey may lack solid ground or a plan,
But laughs echo loud from a shadowy span.
With every odd step on this endless parade,
I find joy in the vague, and I'm never afraid!

Labyrinth of Thought

In a maze of my own design,
Thoughts race like squirrels on caffeine,
Left turns and right, oh where's the sign?
It's all quite absurd, yet so routine.

I ponder my purpose while sipping my tea,
Do I need a map or just a good friend?
These questions swirl, oh where could they be?
I laugh at the chaos, it has no end.

An epiphany strikes, but it slips like a chance,
Like trying to catch smoke, it just floats away,
I wave at my brain in a chaotic dance,
Maybe tomorrow, I'll join in the fray.

So here I am, stuck in this loop,
Who knew overthinking could be so much fun?
I'll grab some popcorn, make my own scoop,
And watch as my mind races, on the run.

Whispers of the Wandering Mind

My brain is a party, with guests galore,
Each one has a story that's half-hashed and frail,
They chatter and giggle, always wanting more,
While I'm stuck in my chair, just trying to regale.

Thoughts flit like butterflies, bright and aloof,
They dance on the edge of a random idea,
Then zip out the window, poof! What's the proof?
I chase after echoes—'Is that a new fear?'

There's wisdom in nonsense, or so they all claim,
A punchline for meaning, a riddle for fun,
But I spill my secrets like food on a flame,
And watch as they sizzle, leaving me stunned.

So here's to the whispers that make up my night,
To the quirk of my thoughts, a whimsical track,
Though they may seem heavy, they're oddly light,
In the carnival mind, there's simply no lack.

The Weight of Being

I woke up today, with gravity's grip,
Like my brain was a rock, too heavy to hold,
My coffee was lacking, a little bit stripped,
Am I breathing or pondering, honestly told?

So I ponder the purpose of all that's around,
Do penguins get lost in their own waddle?
As thoughts tumble 'round, no answers abound,
I laugh at my musings, it's utter coddle.

With the weight of my thoughts pressing down like a lead,

Do fish grip the water, or is it just free?
I scribble my worries, at least I am fed,
In this circus of life, it's quite funny to be.

So let's celebrate life, with its ups and its downs,
A balancing act on this tightrope we tread,
In the chaos of thinking, I wear silly crowns,
And jesterly ponderings dance in my head.

Intersections of Time

At the corner of now and the avenue then,
I trip over moments like a clueless mime,
With clocks that tick loudly, forcing me again,
To wonder what's lost in the shadows of time.

I met my past self; we laughed—what a sight!
"Remember that haircut?" I gleefully said.
But future me winked, with a wild kind of light,
"You'll look back, and realize it's all just a thread."

In the tapestry woven, each strand has a tale,
Like socks in the dryer, maybe spinning alone,
Yet laughter unites us, through joy and through pale,
In a world full of question marks carved into stone.

So, I'll dance at the junction where past meets the now,
In the fabric of moments all lined with a smile,
Time's an awkward parent; I'm just learning how,
To navigate life's maze, it's all worth the while.

Searching for Wholeness

I searched for my other sock,
But all I found was dust.
Is this my life's great plan?
Or just an existential bust?

I asked a mirror for advice,
It just cracked a smile back.
"Do you ever feel alone?"
"No," said it, "I'm full of cracks!"

I tried to find my missing piece,
Under the couch, and in my shoe.
But maybe I'm already whole,
Just in a puzzle made for two.

In the end, I've come to see,
Wholeness is just a state of mind.
Like mixing chips in my ice cream,
You'll find joy in being blind.

Tides of Transience

Life's like a beach ball on the sea,
It bounces and rolls, but doesn't flee.
Caught between waves of joy and grief,
I laugh through my own disbelief.

Each moment is a splash in time,
Like sand castles that start to climb.
Then swoosh! They're gone with the next tide,
Just quick delights we can't abide.

I tried to catch a moment's kiss,
It slipped through my fingers; what a miss!
Is this the game of life's delight?
To chase shadows by day and night?

Still, I dance upon the shore,
With silly moves I can't ignore.
For every wave that washes away,
I'm here to play another day!

Reflections in a Broken Mirror

A mirror cracked, a face in shards,
Each piece shows me juggling cards.
Am I the clown or just the jest?
In broken bits, I feel the best.

I'm laughing at my own wild hair,
Who needs a comb? I don't care!
With each reflection, I see a clue,
Life's a comedy, and I'm the crew.

I tried to fix my crooked smile,
But it grew on me after a while.
In every flaw, there's a story told,
A spark of fun in the bold and cold.

I learned to love my jagged face,
Imperfections add a funny grace.
So here's to laughs in every line,
In this shattered world, I'm a divine!

Echo Chambers of the Soul

I whispered to my inner voice,
It echoed back a bad choice.
"Why'd you try to dance today?"
"Because it's fun, and I'm not gray!"

In chambers deep where thoughts collide,
I hear my doubts they can't abide.
"Who needs adventure?" they all cry,
"Just stay in bed, don't even try!"

But suddenly, a giggle blooms,
As I break out from dreary rooms.
What if I wear mismatched shoes?
Life gets colorful with crazy hues!

So here's to echoes that turn loud,
In the laughter of the inner crowd.
For even in the noise they bring,
My soul finds joy in everything!

Memories of a Dream Unraveled

Last night I soared, hey, I was a bird,
But morning came, and I forgot the word.
I flew through skies made of cotton candy,
Now I'm awake, and it feels quite dandy.

I danced with shadows in a neon haze,
But reality pulled me from my daze.
Where's my cape, my crown, my fancy shoes?
Oh well, guess I'm still in my PJs, snooze!

In twisted worlds where llamas can sing,
I chased wild dreams and butterflies' wings.
But here I am, just staring at toast,
Was it all real, or did I just boast?

Yet in this chaos, I laugh and I muse,
For life's a joke, and I'm here to choose.
So cheers to dreams that unpredictably wane,
I'll wear my PJs and dance in the rain.

Reflections on a Shattered Mirror

In pieces I see, oh, what a sight,
My hair's a mess, and my shirt's too tight.
Who is that face, all crooked and strange?
Must be my twin, oh, isn't that deranged?

Each shard holds a tale, a joke gone awry,
Like when I tried to bake and set off a sigh.
The smoke alarm sings, a true melody,
Who knew canines could be such critics, you see?

I grin at my flaws, each crack is a laugh,
That time I tripped on the sidewalk, oh my gaff!
With giggles and snorts, I dance on my way,
Embracing the chaos, it's just another day.

So here I stand, in this fractured glee,
With mirrored reflections quite silly and free.
Life's just a puzzle we put in a whirl,
Thank goodness for laughter to brighten my world.

Embracing the Silence of Doubt

In quiet moments, my brain does a flip,
Why'd I load my schedule like a sinking ship?
I ponder the purpose of socks left alone,
In the laundromat lost, they quietly moan.

Should I take the leap, or just take a nap?
Life's big questions feel like a trap.
Yet here in the silence, I peek and I pry,
Like a cat with a laser, oh my, oh my!

Is the fridge aware of its role as a muse?
It hums like a tune, quite the comic ruse.
While contemplating cheese, I ponder and pout,
Embracing this silence while sipping my stout.

So here I float in this sea of my thoughts,
Waffling wildly through all they have taught.
I chuckle and sigh as I sit with my fate,
Knowing silence, too, can be wonderfully great.

When Time Stood Still

Once upon a moment, I found a lost clock,
Ticking so slowly, it felt like a rock.
I stared at my phone, still scrolling in dread,
Wondering if I'd find the snacks I had spread.

In frozen tranquility, I missed my cue,
Was that a bird or just a shoe?
As seconds unravel in a comedic race,
I laugh at the chaos, it's quite the embrace.

With time in a twist, I twirled with delight,
Each second a giggle that felt just right.
I took a long breath, and then guess what,
Time decided to move, oh, what a plot!

But in the frenzy of moments I chase,
I found joy in silliness, my saving grace.
So here's to those pauses when life feels sublime,
Raise a toast to the madness, let's savor the time!

Interlude in a World Unraveled

My socks shout rebellion each day,
Left alone, right goes astray,
The microwave's beep, a siren's song,
As I ponder where I went wrong.

Me and my coffee, a chaotic pair,
It spills on my plans, an unwelcome affair,
The clock ticks loud, like a drumline's beat,
Yet I sit here lost, in a dance with my seat.

The cat in the window, she looks quite wise,
Watching my antics with half-closed eyes,
I wonder if she knows the secret code,
To conquer this life, or just to explode.

A sandwich I made, with existential dread,
Pickles of doubt, on the learning bread,
I take a big bite, as if it will clear,
All of the thoughts, that bubble with fear.

Voices of the Inner Conflagration

In my head, a circus, clowns on parade,
Juggling my worries, a big charade,
The lion roars, that's just my mind,
A contest of chaos, surreal and unkind.

Disco on Tuesdays, the theme's been set,
Dance with my worries, but they're not quite met,
The floor is my heart, it's spinning so fast,
With every misstep, it's a painful blast.

My thoughts keep whispering, plotting their scheme,
"Why did you eat that? Was it truly a dream?"
Cupcakes of guilt, sprinkling confusion,
In this wild brain food, there's no resolution.

Oh to be a goldfish, swimming so free,
Forgetful of purpose, just happy to be,
But I'm stuck with this noggin, it's a heavy weight,
As I juggle my thoughts, and contemplate fate.

Between Existence and Absence

I exist in my chair, a plush throne of fluff,
Wrestling with silence, it's all just too tough,
The fridge hums a tune, quite soothing indeed,
As I ponder my life choices over some seed.

Behind me, my thoughts play hide and seek,
"Where are you going?" I shout with a squeak,
They laugh as they scatter, evading my grasp,
In the game of existence, I'm left in the rasp.

Naps are my passion, a fleeting delight,
Though they never answer the questions at night,
Should I bake a pie, or just binge on a show?
Between all the options, my brain moves so slow.

But then there's the joy, of socks that don't match,
A palette of chaos, I've found my own catch,
In this wild journey, I'm a jester at best,
Dancing with shadows, in a colorful jest.

Chasing Shadows in a Distant Light

I chase my own shadow, it giggles and runs,
Dodging my questions like mischievous puns,
With each step I take, it's a two-step ahead,
While I grumble and ponder, just wishing for bread.

Light bulbs flicker, my thoughts play the fool,
"Do you really need purpose?" they laugh, oh so cool,
As I twirl in a dance with my existential gloom,
The walls whisper secrets, they echo in my room.

I trip on my dreams, they wander too wide,
And my laundry piles high, a colorful tide,
Yet still, there's a flicker of something so bright,
In chasing these shadows, I find my own light.

Perhaps in this chaos, there's laughter to find,
A comedy sketch of the curious mind,
So here's to the chase, and what comes in between,
In the game of existence, I'll laugh like a queen.

www.ingramcontent.com/pod-product-compliance
Lightning Source LLC
Chambersburg PA
CBHW071825160426
43209CB00003B/209